PRESIDENT ROOSEVELT'S
FIRST AND SECOND NEW DEALS

GREAT DEPRESSION FOR KIDS

History Book 5th Grade | Children's History

Speedy Publishing LLC
40 E. Main St. #1156
Newark, DE 19711
www.speedypublishing.com

In this book, we're going to talk about President Franklin D. Roosevelt's First and Second New Deals. So, let's get right to it!

After the Stock Market Crash of 1929, the Great Depression began. The economy of the United States was in chaos. Thousands of banks had gone bankrupt and over 30% of the population was out of work. The happy, carefree years of the *"Roaring Twenties"* were over. After the crash, Herbert Hoover, who had become president in 1929 a few

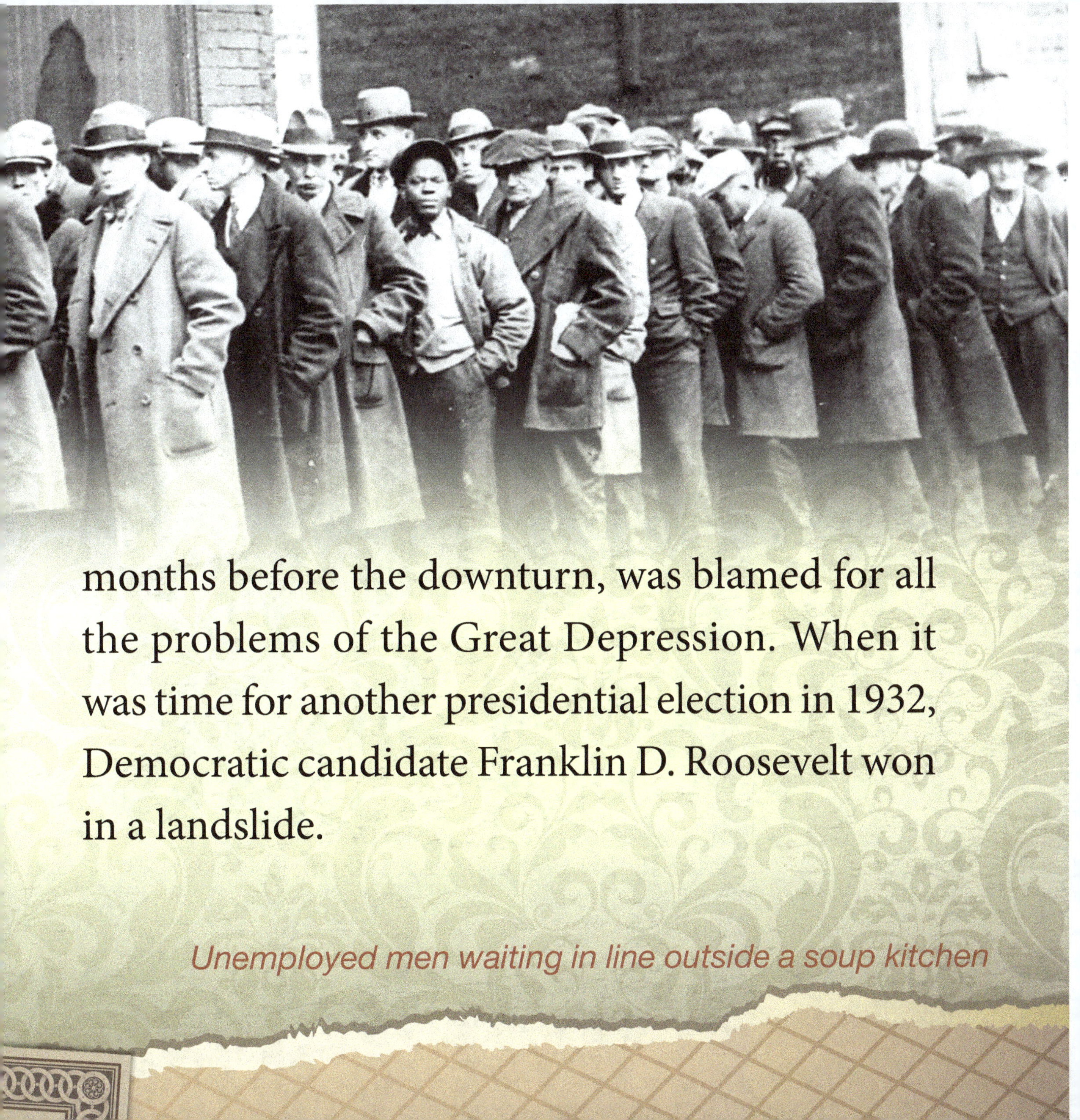

months before the downturn, was blamed for all the problems of the Great Depression. When it was time for another presidential election in 1932, Democratic candidate Franklin D. Roosevelt won in a landslide.

Unemployed men waiting in line outside a soup kitchen

Roosevelt signing TVA Act (1933).

The programs that Roosevelt put into place were called the *"New Deal."* The programs he established from 1932 to 1935 were called the *"First New Deal"* and the ones after 1935 were part of the *"Second New Deal."*

THE FIRST NEW DEAL

The *"First New Deal"* included laws to reform banking, to repeal Prohibition, and to create public works projects.

Hardwick Vermont streets with campaign signs for 'Roosevelt and Garner' 'The Townsend Plan' and Landon and Knox. Sept. 1936.

ELT AND GARNER
IT IS UP TO YOU TO
IT ENACTED THIS LAW
FOR IT   VOTE FOR IT
KNOX
DRUGS

THE FIRST HUNDRED DAYS OF ROOSEVELT'S ADMINISTRATION

Roosevelt was a man of action and he had promised the American people that he would make sure that the *"forgotten man"* wasn't forgotten any longer. By this he meant that he fully understood the suffering they had undergone and would take speedy action to alleviate it. As soon as he was sworn in as president, he started to get things moving quickly.

Stock traders on the floor of the New York Stock Exchange in 1936.

He issued executive orders and persuaded Congress to pass some of his proposed laws without delay.

He also did something that no other president had ever done. He began talking to the American people on the radio to tell them what he was doing to help make conditions better.

Roosevelt's fireside chat on the merits of the recovery program (June 28, 1934).

His speeches, called *"fireside chats,"* were written and spoken in a friendly tone and told the listeners exactly what he was planning to do step-by-step and why he was planning to do it. This direct *"conversation"* with the public did much to alleviate people's fears and concerns.

REFORMING THE BANKING INDUSTRY

One of the first actions Roosevelt took was to shut down all the United States banks for four days. This forced *"bank holiday"* gave him time to have the banks inspected to see if they were financially stable before they were reopened. This *"holiday"* gave Congress time to take action.

Crowds in the lobby of a Detroit Bank.

During the shutdown, Congress quickly passed the Emergency Banking Relief Act. The Act allowed the Federal Reserve Banks to ensure that there was enough money when the banks reopened.

Prior to this time, there had been so many bank runs that the entire banking system was on the verge of collapsing. A bank run is when all the customers for a particular bank show up at the same time to withdraw their funds.

Roosevelt had explained how banking works during his first fireside chat. He told the American people that banks invested their monies and didn't keep their cash in a vault. If everyone tried to cash out their money at the same time, the bank would not have enough liquid assets to cover it. He also explained to them that their money was safer in a bank than anywhere else.

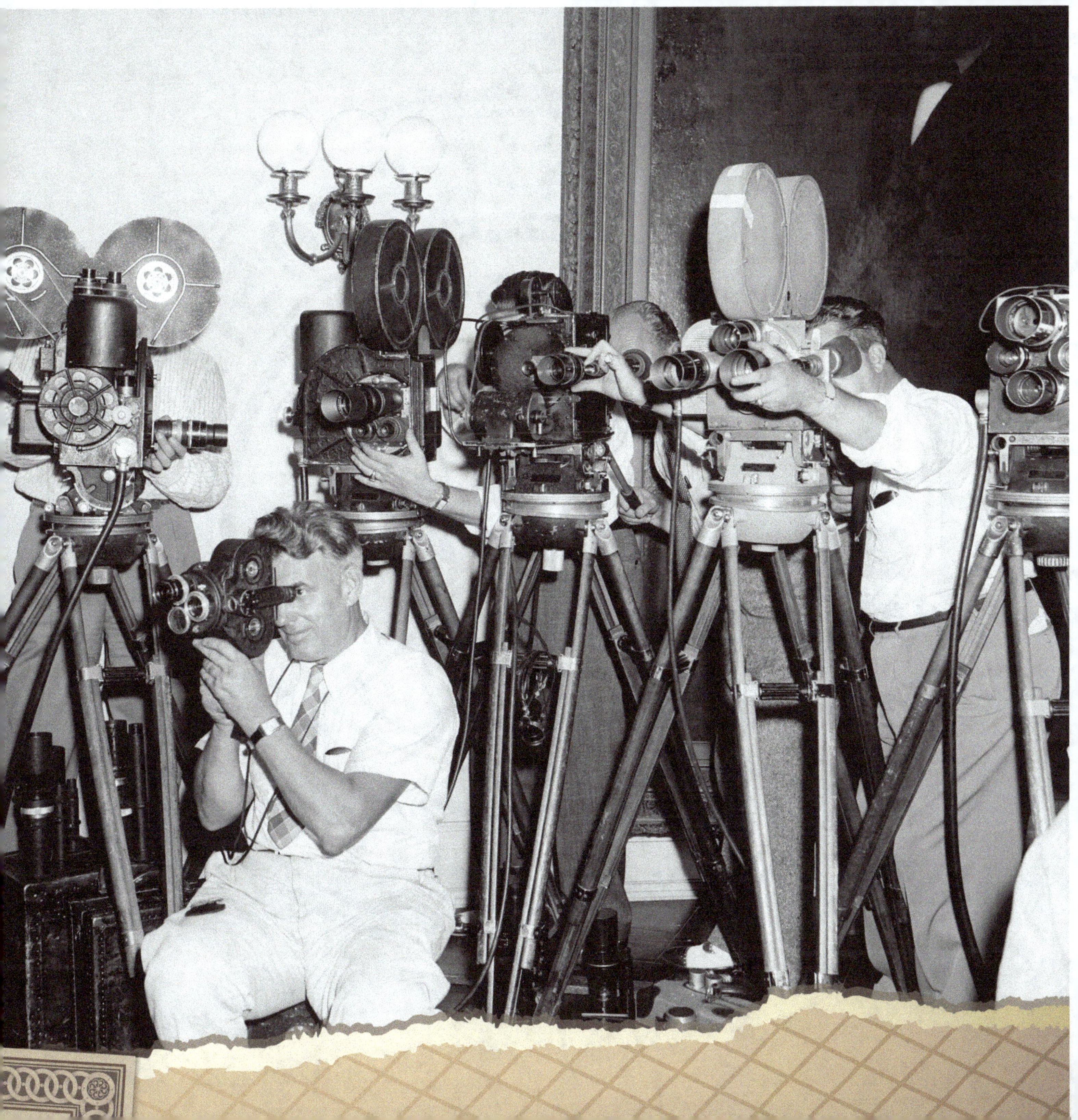

FEDERAL DEPOSIT
INSURANCE CORPORATION
1933

When the banks reopened, the customers came back and returned more than half of the savings they had previously withdrawn during the time of the bank runs. Eventually, the 1933 Emergency Banking Act was extended to include the Federal Deposit Insurance Corporation or FDIC. The FDIC now guarantees individual savings accounts to a certain amount so that a person's savings are insured by the government and can't just disappear.

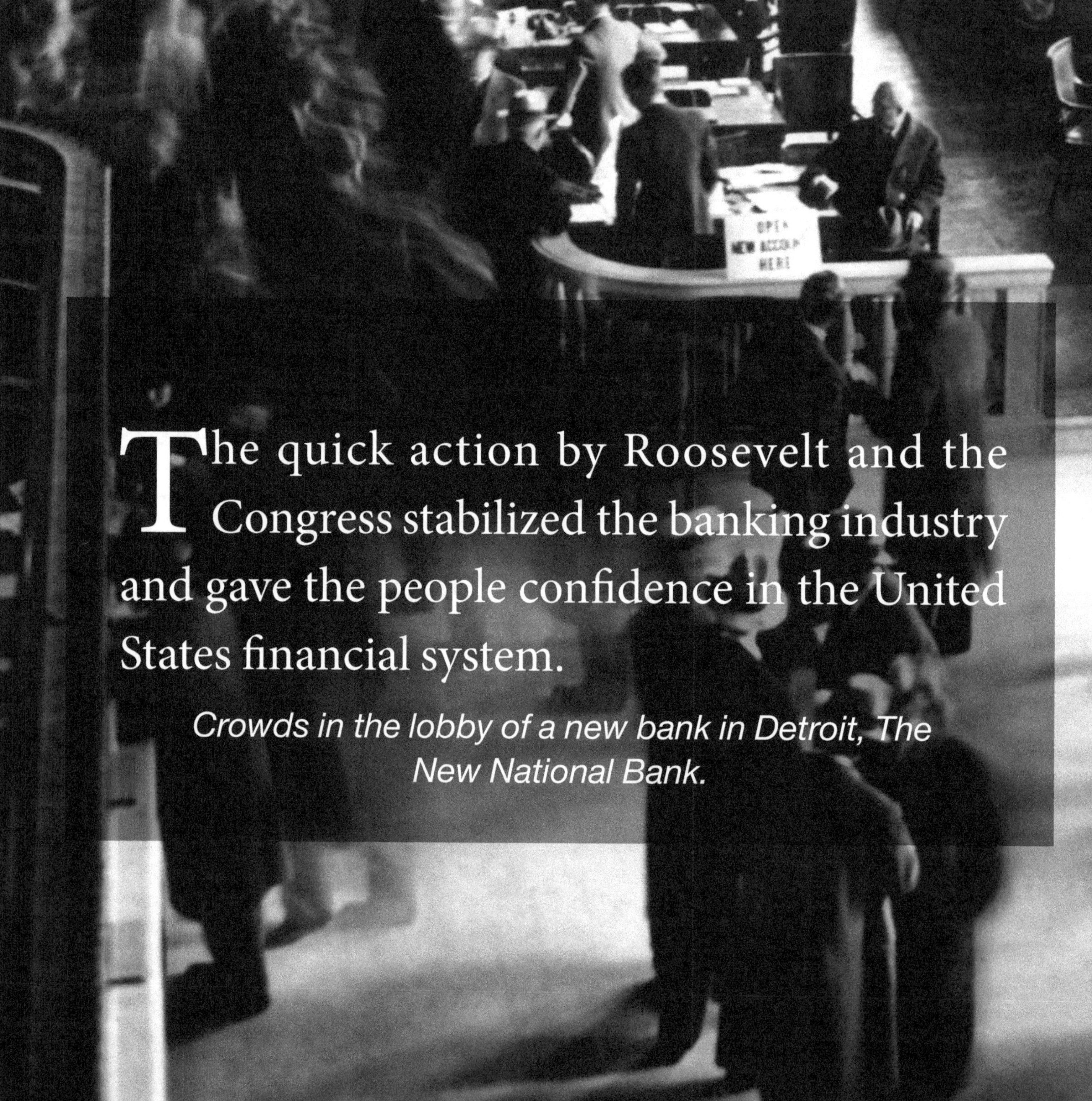

The quick action by Roosevelt and the Congress stabilized the banking industry and gave the people confidence in the United States financial system.

Crowds in the lobby of a new bank in Detroit, The New National Bank.

OPEN
NEW ACCOUNTS
HERE
TEMPORARY
QUARTERS
NATIONAL BANK
of DETROIT

The Federal Government offered loans to Veterans for transportation home and food

THE SECURITIES ACT OF 1933

Next on the agenda was the passing of the Securities Act. This Act made it necessary for companies that were traded on the stock market to be transparent in their dealings with the public. They were required to provide correct information regarding the amounts of their losses as well as profits. They also had to provide information regarding the corporate leaders of their companies.

THE END OF PROHIBITION

Prohibition had been in place in the United States since 1920. It had made the production, transportation, and sale of alcohol illegal. It had been a miserable failure. People still wanted to drink alcoholic beverages so they did it illegally and a lot of people were breaking the law. Also, career criminals got into the sale of alcohol so Prohibition caused a lot of crime.

Crowd of applicants at Broad of Health for permits to sell beer in NYC, April 6, 1933.

Repeal
The
18th
Amendment
The Crusaders

The President repealed prohibition until the 21st Amendment to the Constitution could formally repeal it. It wasn't illegal to serve or drink alcohol anymore and this change made people happy and also brought in tax revenue.

'Repeal the 18th Amendment' slogan on a spare tire cover. Dec. 16, 1930.

Next, President Roosevelt created an organization called the Public Works Administration or PWA for short. Through this group, he began programs to put people to work by building or repairing the transportation systems in the United States, such as roads and bridges. There were also programs to repair dams, schools, and hospitals.

Road construction workers, in the 1930s.

MERANDO CO.
BUILDERS
WASHINGTON. D.C.
P.W.A.
FEDERAL WORKS AGENCY
PUBLIC WORKS ADMINISTRATION
RECORDER OF DEEDS, D.C. BLDG.
PROJECT NO. D.C. 1034 F
ATLAS EXCAVATING
LORAIN DIESEL

This put many men to work and helped fix the crumbling infrastructure of the United States. Another group, called the CCC or Civilian Conservation Corps created jobs working at the national parks and monuments.

FARM PROGRAMS

The AAA or Agricultural Adjustment Administration was created to help United States farmers. It helped them to use better farming techniques, it put controls on the amounts that farms could produce so that prices would stabilize and rise, and it gave farmers a say in the way they would be governed.

Men and mules cultivating cotton at the Lake Dick Cooperative Association farm.

Depression era slums in Washington D.C.

Great Depression Hooverville in lower Manhattan. 1932.

HOUSING

Many homes had been foreclosed during the Depression. So many people had lost their homes that they were living in shanty towns that were called *"Hoovervilles"* after the previous president, Herbert Hoover. Roosevelt formed the Home Owners' Loan Corporation, called HOLC for short, as well as the Federal Housing Administration or FHA.

The HOLC was established so that people who had kept their homes could refinance their mortgages and get lower payments. The primary goal of the FHA was to establish construction standards for homes so that they would be safe for people to live in. These measures helped to stabilize the housing market.

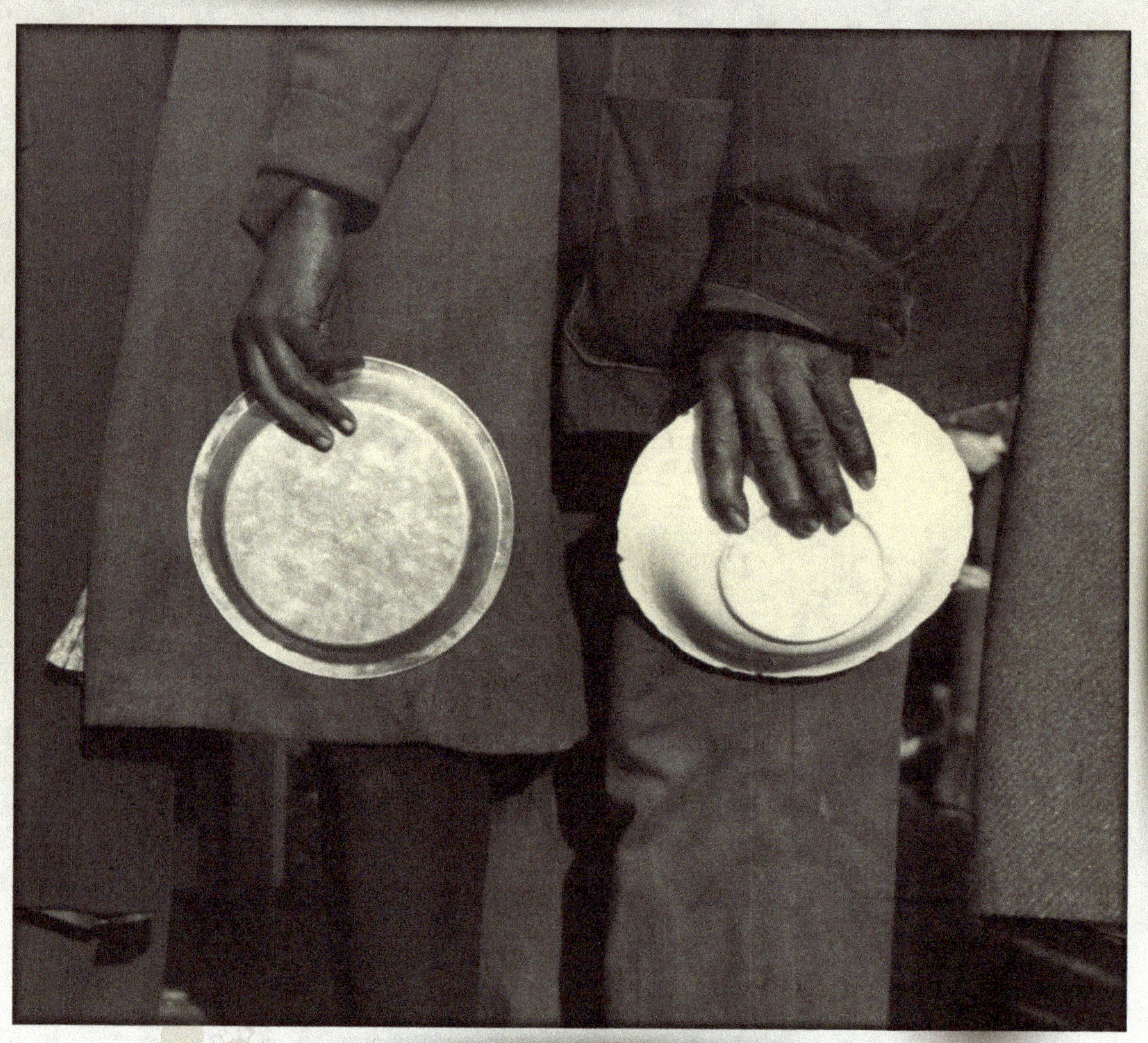

African Americans in the lineup for food.

EMERGENCY RELIEF

It was going to take time for people to get back on their feet again. The Federal Emergency Relief Administration offered assistance to people who were jobless. It created soup kitchens for supplying food for the hungry and gave blankets to homeless people. It also created school lunch programs so children would eat during the day and helped educate unemployed people on how to seek new jobs.

THE SECOND NEW DEAL

Despite everything that had been done in the First New Deal, the Great Depression continued and there didn't seem to be any relief in sight. In 1935, Roosevelt decided to pass more laws to help fix the economic problems. These laws were called the *"Second New Deal."*

Chamber of Commerce
Tenino, Wash.
ONE DOLLAR

MORE SECURITY FOR
THE AMERICAN FAMILY
THE SOCIAL SECURITY ACT AS AMENDED
OFFERS GREATER OLD-AGE INSURANCE
PROTECTION TO PEOPLE NOW NEARING
RETIREMENT AGE.
FOR INFORMATION WRITE OR CALL AT THE NEAREST FIELD OFFICE OF THE
SOCIAL SECURITY BOARD

SOCIAL SECURITY

One of the most important acts passed during this time was the Social Security Act. This Act was designed to help people who were retired or unable to work. It provided payments for retirees as well as orphans and those who were disabled. These benefits were paid for by the institution of a payroll tax that was split between the employers and the workers.

1930s poster publicizing the benefits available to elderly Americans under the new Social Security programs.

WORKS PROGRESS ADMINISTRATION

The WPA, which stood for Works Progress Administration, was formed. This government organization recruited jobless workers to construct various public works projects, such as the building of airports and schools as well as roads and bridges. During the Depression, the WPA placed 8 million workers in jobs.

An idle plow on farm land adjacent to eroded land in Jackson County Alabama. The New Deal established agricultural education programs.

Telephone operators working on an international switchboard in the 1930s.

LABOR RELATIONS

Congress passed the National Labor Relations Act in 1935. This Act ensured specific rights for unions and their workers. It also established a board run by the federal government to negotiate and arbitrate any disagreements between workers and their employers in terms of wages or working conditions. Three years later, the Fair Labor Standards Act was passed.

$\mathbf{T}$his law mandated that workers shouldn't work more than 44 hours per week and that their minimum wage shouldn't be lower than 25 cents hourly. It also prohibited children from working.

U.S.
RESETTLEMENT
ADMINISTRATION
PROJECT NUMBER LD-FL-3
REGION NUMBER-V
CONSERVING 115,000 ACRES
FOR FOREST, WILDLIFE,
PASTURE AND RECREATION

HOUSING

In 1937, the Housing Authority was established. This agency was responsible for tearing down the Depression slums and finding solutions for housing the homeless.

US Resettlement Administration sign for the Withlacoochee Land Use Project.

DID THE FIRST AND SECOND NEW DEALS STOP THE DEPRESSION?

Historians and economists have many different views on whether Roosevelt's programs were successful or not. The reason is that the economy didn't improve significantly until the beginning of the Second World War in 1939. Factories and factory workers were needed to fight the war and this change improved the economy. Many people believe that the programs Roosevelt put into position are still needed to maintain a strong

national economy. In any case, Roosevelt's New Deals had a major impact on the nation during the dark times of the Great Depression and they are still significant today.

JOBLESS ENGLAND
LESS DREAD
FIGHT AGAINST FORECLOSURE SMALL HOMES
#24
UNEMPLOYED COUNCIL
DOWN WITH WAR!
WE DEMAND CASH RELIEF
EMPLOYED WORKERS
VOTE NOV 8
WITHDRAW FROM CHINA

A wesome! Now you know more about President Roosevelt's New Deals. You can find more History books from Baby Professor by searching the website of your favorite book retailer.

Visit
BABY PROFESSOR
EDUCATION KIDS
www.BabyProfessorBooks.com
to download Free Baby Professor eBooks
and view our catalog of new and exciting
Children's Books